Preface

Welcome to the CTET Paper 2 Class VI to VIII Social Science Book!

Teaching is a journey of learning, discovery, and personal growth. This book is designed to support you on that journey as you prepare for the Central Teacher Eligibility Test (CTET). Whether you are an aspiring educator or looking to enhance your knowledge, this book will equip you with essential concepts, strategies, and insights to excel in the exam and in your future teaching career.

Our goal is to make your learning experience meaningful and effective. Each chapter in this book has been carefully crafted to engage both your curiosity and critical thinking, covering core topics essential for the CTET exam. Along the way, you will find opportunities to reflect on best practices in education, the role of teachers in shaping society, and the importance of fostering an inclusive and supportive learning environment.

Table of Contents

Chapter 1: Questions

1.**Where did the earliest human societies first appear?**
a) Europe
b) Africa
c) Asia
d) North America
Answer: b

2.**What was the primary occupation of the first farmers?**
a) Hunting
b) Agriculture
c) Trading
d) Pottery
Answer: b

3.**Which was one of the earliest cities in the world?**
a) Athens
b) Rome
c) Mohenjo-Daro
d) London
Answer: c

4.**Which dynasty established the first empire in India?**
a) Maurya Empire
b) Gupta Empire
c) Mughal Empire
d) Chola Empire
Answer: a

5.**Which king built the Great Stupa at Sanchi?**
a) Chandragupta
b) Ashoka
c) Harsha
d) Akbar
Answer: b

6.**What was the primary focus of early states in history?**
a) Art
b) Agriculture
c) Trade and governance
d) Religion
Answer: c

7.**Which religion originated during the early state period in India?**
a) Hinduism
b) Jainism
c) Christianity
d) Islam
Answer: b

8.**Which empire is known for spreading Buddhism beyond India?**
a) Maurya Empire
b) Gupta Empire
c) Mughal Empire
d) British Empire
Answer: a

9.**What was a significant result of the revolt of 1857?**
a) End of the East India Company's rule
b) Beginning of British colonialism
c) Establishment of Mughal rule
d) Industrialization of India
Answer: a

10.**Which reformer fought for women's education in colonial India?**
a) Raja Ram Mohan Roy
b) Mahatma Gandhi
c) Subhash Chandra Bose
d) Rabindranath Tagore
Answer: a

11.**Which year marked India's independence?**
a) 1945
b) 1947
c) 1950
d) 1948
Answer: b

12.**What is the shape of the Earth?**
a) Perfect sphere
b) Oblate spheroid
c) Flat disc
d) Ellipse
Answer: b

13.**Which planet is known as the 'Blue Planet'?**
a) Mars
b) Jupiter
c) Earth
d) Neptune
Answer: c

14.**What is the primary gas in Earth's atmosphere?**
a) Oxygen
b) Carbon dioxide
c) Nitrogen
d) Hydrogen
Answer: c

15.**Which layer of the atmosphere contains the ozone layer?**
a) Troposphere
b) Stratosphere
c) Mesosphere
d) Thermosphere
Answer: b

16.**What is the largest source of fresh water on Earth?**
a) Rivers
b) Lakes
c) Glaciers
d) Groundwater
Answer: c

17.**Which resource is renewable?**
a) Coal
b) Petroleum
c) Solar energy
d) Natural gas
Answer: c

18.**Which crop is known as a cash crop?**
a) Wheat
b) Rice
c) Cotton
d) Barley
Answer: c

19.**What is the primary function of local government?**
a) Maintain international relations
b) Enforce national laws
c) Manage community services and development
d) Control national security
Answer: c

20.**What is the basic principle of democracy?**
a) Rule by a king
b) Rule by elected representatives
c) Rule by military power
d) Rule by divine authority
Answer: b

21.**What is the primary function of media in a democracy?**
a) Promote propaganda
b) Provide entertainment
c) Inform citizens and hold power accountable
d) Support specific political parties
Answer: c

22.**Which part of the constitution guarantees fundamental rights?**
a) Preamble
b) Fundamental Rights Chapter
c) Directive Principles of State Policy
d) Citizenship Act
Answer: b

23.**What is the term for government by representatives?**
a) Democracy
b) Autocracy
c) Monarchy
d) Republic
Answer: d

24.**What is the highest court of appeal in India?**
a) High Court
b) District Court
c) Supreme Court
d) Magistrate's Court
Answer: c

25.**Which social reformer is known for the abolition of Sati?**
a) Bal Gangadhar Tilak
b) Raja Ram Mohan Roy
c) Jawaharlal Nehru
d) Dr. B.R. Ambedkar
Answer: b

26.**What is the purpose of parliamentary government?**
a) To control all branches of government
b) To ensure power-sharing between the executive and legislature
c) To establish a dictatorship
d) To reduce citizen involvement in governance
Answer: b

27.**What is the nature of social science?**
a) Study of natural phenomena
b) Study of human behavior and society
c) Study of chemical processes
d) Study of astronomical bodies
Answer: b

28.**What encourages critical thinking in students?**
a) Rote memorization
b) Inquiry-based learning
c) Multiple-choice questions only
d) Dictation method
Answer: b

29.**What is a primary source in historical research?**
a) Textbooks
b) Newspaper articles
c) Original letters and documents
d) Encyclopedias
Answer: c

30.**Which method is most effective in teaching social science?**
a) Lecture method
b) Activity-based learning
c) Memorization of dates
d) Copying notes
Answer: b

31.**What is the main focus of project work in social science?**
a) Memorizing facts
b) Encouraging practical application and critical thinking
c) Reducing homework
d) Avoiding group activities
Answer: b

32.**What is the meaning of 'secularism'?**
a) Promotion of one religion
b) Absence of religion
c) Equal treatment of all religions
d) State-controlled religion
Answer: c

33.**Which body is responsible for making laws in India?**
a) Judiciary
b) Executive
c) Legislature
d) Military
Answer: c

34.**What is the primary role of the judiciary?**
a) Enforce laws
b) Create laws
c) Interpret and apply laws
d) Manage elections
Answer: c

35.**Which system governs villages in India?**
a) State government
b) Central government
c) Panchayati Raj
d) Military
Answer: c

36.**Who is known as the 'Father of the Indian Constitution'?**
a) Mahatma Gandhi
b) Jawaharlal Nehru
c) Dr. B.R. Ambedkar
d) Sardar Vallabhbhai Patel
Answer: c

37.**Which article of the Indian Constitution abolishes untouchability?**
a) Article 17
b) Article 21
c) Article 32
d) Article 14
Answer: a

38.**What is the importance of diversity in a society?**
a) It promotes uniformity
b) It fosters tolerance and understanding
c) It causes conflict
d) It limits cultural development
Answer: b

39.**Which river is called the 'Lifeline of India'?**
a) Yamuna
b) Brahmaputra
c) Ganga
d) Narmada
Answer: c

40.**What is the primary aim of education in a democracy?**
a) Promote rote learning
b) Encourage critical thinking and responsible citizenship
c) Create obedient citizens
d) Limit student participation
Answer: b

41.**Which event marked the beginning of the Revolt of 1857?**
a) Partition of Bengal
b) Introduction of the new Enfield rifle
c) Formation of the Indian National Congress
d) Jallianwala Bagh massacre
Answer: b

42.**Which Mughal emperor built the Taj Mahal?**
a) Akbar
b) Jahangir
c) Shah Jahan
d) Aurangzeb
Answer: c

43.**What is the capital of the Mughal Empire during Akbar's reign?**
a) Agra
b) Delhi
c) Fatehpur Sikri
d) Lahore
Answer: c

44.**Which Portuguese explorer discovered the sea route to India?**
a) Christopher Columbus
b) Vasco da Gama
c) Ferdinand Magellan
d) Amerigo Vespucci
Answer: b

45.**Which company established colonial power in India?**
a) Dutch East India Company
b) British East India Company
c) French East India Company
d) Portuguese East India Company
Answer: b

46.**Which year did India become a republic?**
a) 1947
b) 1948
c) 1950
d) 1951
Answer: c

47.**What was the primary reason for the partition of Bengal in 1905?**
a) Administrative convenience
b) Divide and rule policy
c) Religious harmony
d) Industrial development
Answer: b

48.**Which leader gave the call for 'Do or Die' during the Quit India Movement?**
a) Subhash Chandra Bose
b) Jawaharlal Nehru
c) Mahatma Gandhi
d) Bhagat Singh
Answer: c

49.**Which river is known as the 'Sorrow of Bihar'?**
a) Yamuna
b) Kosi
c) Ganga
d) Brahmaputra
Answer: b

50.**Which Indian state is the largest producer of wheat?**
a) Punjab
b) Haryana
c) Uttar Pradesh
d) Madhya Pradesh
Answer: c

51.**Which layer of the Earth contains tectonic plates?**
a) Crust
b) Mantle
c) Outer core
d) Inner core
Answer: a

52.**Which season occurs when the Earth is tilted towards the Sun?**
a) Winter
b) Summer
c) Autumn
d) Spring
Answer: b

53.**Which gas is a major contributor to the greenhouse effect?**
a) Nitrogen
b) Carbon dioxide
c) Oxygen
d) Helium
Answer: b

54.**What is the process of water turning into vapor called?**
a) Condensation
b) Evaporation
c) Precipitation
d) Freezing
Answer: b

55.**What is the importance of panchayats in rural areas?**
a) Provide defense services
b) Manage local governance and development
c) Implement national policies directly
d) Conduct national elections
Answer: b

56.**What is the main source of income for the Indian government?**
a) Corporate taxes
b) Agriculture
c) Income taxes
d) Foreign aid
Answer: c

57.**Which body controls the functioning of media in India?**
a) Press Council of India
b) Election Commission
c) Judiciary
d) Central Bureau of Investigation
Answer: a

58.**What is the primary function of the legislature?**
a) Implement laws
b) Interpret laws
c) Make laws
d) Enforce laws
Answer: c

59.**Which state in India is known for the Sundarbans?**
a) Kerala
b) West Bengal
c) Assam
d) Odisha
Answer: b

60.**What does GDP stand for?**
a) Gross Domestic Product
b) General Development Policy
c) Global Distribution Program
d) Government Development Plan
Answer: a

61.**Which mountain range separates Europe and Asia?**
a) Alps
b) Ural
c) Himalayas
d) Andes
Answer: b

62.**Which organ of the government ensures laws are followed?**
a) Judiciary
b) Executive
c) Legislature
d) Election Commission
Answer: b

63.**What type of farming involves growing crops for personal use?**
a) Subsistence farming
b) Commercial farming
c) Plantation farming
d) Organic farming
Answer: a

64.**What is the importance of the Directive Principles of State Policy?**
a) They are legally enforceable
b) They guide the government in policymaking
c) They restrict individual rights
d) They are binding on citizens
Answer: b

65.**Which Indian city is known as the 'Silicon Valley of India'?**
a) Mumbai
b) Chennai
c) Hyderabad
d) Bengaluru
Answer: d

66.**Which natural disaster is measured using the Richter scale?**
a) Cyclones
b) Floods
c) Earthquakes
d) Tsunamis
Answer: c

67.**Who was the first President of independent India?**
a) Dr. B.R. Ambedkar
b) Jawaharlal Nehru
c) Dr. Rajendra Prasad
d) Sardar Vallabhbhai Patel
Answer: c

68.**Which sector employs the largest number of people in India?**
a) Agriculture
b) Industry
c) Services
d) IT
Answer: a

69.**What is the longest river in India?**
a) Yamuna
b) Godavari
c) Brahmaputra
d) Ganga
Answer: d

70.**Which Article of the Indian Constitution guarantees equality before law?**
a) Article 14
b) Article 17
c) Article 19
d) Article 21
Answer: a

71.**What is the main occupation in rural India?**
a) Industry
b) Agriculture
c) Trade
d) Services
Answer: b

72.**What is the role of the Election Commission in India?**
a) Make laws
b) Implement policies
c) Conduct free and fair elections
d) Manage finances
Answer: c

73.**Which Indian state has the largest forest cover?**
a) Madhya Pradesh
b) Assam
c) Kerala
d) Odisha
Answer: a

74.**Which festival is known as the 'Festival of Lights'?**
a) Holi
b) Diwali
c) Eid
d) Christmas
Answer: b

75.**What is the significance of the Preamble to the Constitution of India?**
a) It outlines the fundamental duties
b) It describes the ideals and objectives of the Constitution
c) It defines the administrative structure
d) It enforces laws
Answer: b

76.**What is the process of water soaking into the ground called?**
a) Infiltration
b) Evaporation
c) Condensation
d) Precipitation
Answer: a

77.**Who was the first Governor-General of independent India?**
a) Dr. Rajendra Prasad
b) Lord Mountbatten
c) C. Rajagopalachari
d) Jawaharlal Nehru
Answer: b

78.**Which sector contributes the most to India's GDP?**
a) Agriculture
b) Manufacturing
c) Services
d) Mining
Answer: c

79.**Which city is known as the 'Financial Capital of India'?**
a) New Delhi
b) Mumbai
c) Kolkata
d) Chennai
Answer: b

80.**Which act abolished untouchability in India?**
a) Civil Rights Act
b) Untouchability (Offences) Act
c) Right to Equality Act
d) Prevention of Atrocities Act
Answer: b

81.**Which Mughal emperor was known for his policy of religious tolerance?**
a) Babur
b) Akbar
c) Aurangzeb
d) Jahangir
Answer: b

82.**Which social reformer is associated with the Brahmo Samaj?**
a) Dayanand Saraswati
b) Raja Ram Mohan Roy
c) Swami Vivekananda
d) Ishwar Chandra Vidyasagar
Answer: b

83.**What is the capital of India?**
a) Mumbai
b) Chennai
c) Kolkata
d) New Delhi
Answer: d

84.**Which ocean lies to the south of India?**
a) Pacific Ocean
b) Atlantic Ocean
c) Indian Ocean
d) Arctic Ocean
Answer: c

85.**Which state is known as the 'Land of Five Rivers'?**
a) Punjab
b) Haryana
c) Uttar Pradesh
d) Rajasthan
Answer: a

86.**Which Indian leader gave the slogan 'Jai Jawan, Jai Kisan'?**
a) Jawaharlal Nehru
b) Indira Gandhi
c) Lal Bahadur Shastri
d) Mahatma Gandhi
Answer: c

87.**What type of farming involves growing crops for sale?**
a) Subsistence farming
b) Commercial farming
c) Mixed farming
d) Terrace farming
Answer: b

88.**What is the main function of the Election Commission of India?**
a) Conducting elections
b) Making laws
c) Managing political parties
d) Enforcing the constitution
Answer: a

89.**Who was the first Indian woman to become the President of India?**
a) Indira Gandhi
b) Pratibha Patil
c) Sarojini Naidu
d) Sushma Swaraj
Answer: b

90.**Which river is called the 'Ganga of the South'?**
a) Krishna
b) Kaveri
c) Godavari
d) Narmada
Answer: c

91.**Which ancient text is known as the earliest book of India?**
a) Ramayana
b) Mahabharata
c) Rigveda
d) Upanishads
Answer: c

92.**What is the largest democracy in the world?**
a) China
b) USA
c) India
d) Russia
Answer: c

93.**What is the official language of India?**
a) Hindi
b) English
c) Bengali
d) Urdu
Answer: a

94.**Which festival marks the harvest season in Punjab?**
a) Diwali
b) Pongal
c) Baisakhi
d) Onam
Answer: c

95.**Which amendment lowered the voting age in India from 21 to 18?**
a) 42nd Amendment
b) 61st Amendment
c) 44th Amendment
d) 73rd Amendment
Answer: b

96.**Which country shares the longest border with India?**
a) Pakistan
b) China
c) Bangladesh
d) Nepal
Answer: c

97.**What is the significance of the Ashoka Chakra in the Indian flag?**
a) Represents peace
b) Symbolizes courage
c) Denotes progress
d) Reflects the wheel of law
Answer: d

98.**Which mountain pass connects India to China?**
a) Khyber Pass
b) Nathu La Pass
c) Bolan Pass
d) Shipki La Pass
Answer: b

99.**What is the largest desert in India?**
a) Thar Desert
b) Deccan Desert
c) Kutch Desert
d) Ladakh Desert
Answer: a

100.**Which act gave India its independence from British rule?**
a) Government of India Act, 1935
b) Indian Independence Act, 1947
c) Rowlatt Act
d) Civil Rights Act
Answer: b

Chapter 2: Questions

101.**Which state in India has the highest literacy rate?**
a) Kerala
b) Tamil Nadu
c) Maharashtra
d) Karnataka
Answer: a

102.**Who was the first Prime Minister of independent India?**
a) Mahatma Gandhi
b) Jawaharlal Nehru
c) Sardar Vallabhbhai Patel
d) Dr. Rajendra Prasad
Answer: b

103.**What is the term for a seasonal wind that brings heavy rains to India?**
a) Cyclone
b) Monsoon
c) Tornado
d) Typhoon
Answer: b

104.**Which body makes laws at the state level in India?**
a) Lok Sabha
b) Rajya Sabha
c) Legislative Assembly
d) Gram Panchayat
Answer: c

105.**Who was the founder of the Indian National Congress?**
a) Mahatma Gandhi
b) A.O. Hume
c) Bal Gangadhar Tilak
d) Jawaharlal Nehru
Answer: b

106.**Which city is famous for its Charminar?**
a) Delhi
b) Hyderabad
c) Jaipur
d) Lucknow
Answer: b

107.**What is the smallest state in India by area?**
a) Goa
b) Sikkim
c) Tripura
d) Mizoram
Answer: a

108.**What is the term for the cultivation of plants without soil?**
a) Aquaculture
b) Hydroponics
c) Silviculture
d) Horticulture
Answer: b

109.**Which element is used in pencils?**
a) Lead
b) Graphite
c) Charcoal
d) Silicon
Answer: b

110.**What is the oldest mountain range in India?**
a) Himalayas
b) Aravalli Range
c) Vindhya Range
d) Satpura Range
Answer: b

111.**Which act reserved seats for women in local governance?**
a) 61st Amendment
b) 73rd Amendment
c) 42nd Amendment
d) 86th Amendment
Answer: b

112.**What is the capital of Maharashtra?**
a) Pune
b) Mumbai
c) Nagpur
d) Nashik
Answer: b

113.**Which Indian scientist is known as the 'Missile Man of India'?**
a) C.V. Raman
b) Homi Bhabha
c) A.P.J. Abdul Kalam
d) Vikram Sarabhai
Answer: c

114.**Which river flows through the city of Varanasi?**
a) Yamuna
b) Ganga
c) Brahmaputra
d) Godavari
Answer: b

115.**What is the currency of India?**
a) Dollar
b) Pound
c) Rupee
d) Yen
Answer: c

116.**Which temple in Odisha is known for its unique chariot design?**
a) Konark Sun Temple
b) Jagannath Temple
c) Lingaraj Temple
d) Meenakshi Temple
Answer: a

117.**Which state in India is known as the 'Tea Garden of India'?**
a) Assam
b) West Bengal
c) Kerala
d) Tamil Nadu
Answer: a

118.**What is the main objective of the 'Green Revolution'?**
a) Increase industrial production
b) Improve healthcare
c) Increase agricultural productivity
d) Promote education
Answer: c

119.**Which dam is built on the Narmada River?**
a) Bhakra Dam
b) Hirakud Dam
c) Sardar Sarovar Dam
d) Tehri Dam
Answer: c

120.**Which Indian leader popularized the use of the spinning wheel?**
a) Jawaharlal Nehru
b) Mahatma Gandhi
c) Subhash Chandra Bose
d) Bhagat Singh
Answer: b

121.**Which monument in Delhi is known as the symbol of Indian independence?**
a) Red Fort
b) India Gate
c) Qutub Minar
d) Rashtrapati Bhavan
Answer: a

122.**What is the main function of the Rajya Sabha?**
a) Formulate international policies
b) Review and amend laws proposed by the Lok Sabha
c) Implement government programs
d) Enforce the constitution
Answer: b

123.**Who is considered the 'Iron Man of India'?**
a) Mahatma Gandhi
b) Sardar Vallabhbhai Patel
c) Bhagat Singh
d) Subhash Chandra Bose
Answer: b

124.**Which state in India is famous for the Pushkar Camel Fair?**
a) Rajasthan
b) Gujarat
c) Madhya Pradesh
d) Haryana
Answer: a

125.**What is the primary cause of deforestation in India?**
a) Urbanization and agriculture
b) Mining
c) Industrialization
d) Tourism
Answer: a

126.**Which Indian festival celebrates the victory of good over evil?**
a) Diwali
b) Holi
c) Dussehra
d) Pongal
Answer: c

127.**Which Indian port is known as the 'Queen of the Arabian Sea'?**
a) Mumbai
b) Kochi
c) Chennai
d) Visakhapatnam
Answer: b

128.**Which Prime Minister of India was awarded the Bharat Ratna posthumously?**
a) Lal Bahadur Shastri
b) Jawaharlal Nehru
c) Indira Gandhi
d) Rajiv Gandhi
Answer: a

129.**Which Indian river is called the 'River of Sorrows'?**
a) Kosi
b) Brahmaputra
c) Mahanadi
d) Ganga
Answer: a

130.**Which continent is known as the 'Land of Kangaroos'?**
a) Africa
b) South America
c) Australia
d) Asia
Answer: c

131.**What is the capital of Tamil Nadu?**
a) Chennai
b) Madurai
c) Coimbatore
d) Tiruchirappalli
Answer: a

132.**Which Indian mountain pass connects India to Pakistan?**
a) Nathu La Pass
b) Rohtang Pass
c) Khyber Pass
d) Shipki La Pass
Answer: c

133.**What is the longest railway platform in India?**
a) Gorakhpur
b) Kanpur
c) Howrah
d) New Delhi
Answer: a

134.**Which dam in India is built on the Bhagirathi River?**
a) Hirakud Dam
b) Sardar Sarovar Dam
c) Tehri Dam
d) Bhakra Dam
Answer: c

135.**What type of government does India have?**
a) Monarchy
b) Dictatorship
c) Parliamentary democracy
d) Presidential democracy
Answer: c

136.**Which body resolves disputes related to elections in India?**
a) Supreme Court
b) Election Commission
c) Lok Sabha
d) High Court
Answer: a

137.**What is the oldest working port in India?**
a) Chennai Port
b) Mumbai Port
c) Kolkata Port
d) Visakhapatnam Port
Answer: c

138.**Who was the founder of the All India Muslim League?**
a) Muhammad Ali Jinnah
b) Sir Syed Ahmed Khan
c) Agha Khan III
d) Nawab Salimullah
Answer: d

139.**Which state in India is the leading producer of spices?**
a) Kerala
b) Karnataka
c) Tamil Nadu
d) Andhra Pradesh
Answer: a

140.**Which festival marks the start of the harvest season in Tamil Nadu?**
a) Pongal
b) Onam
c) Baisakhi
d) Navratri
Answer: a

141.**Which Indian scientist discovered the Raman Effect?**
a) C.V. Raman
b) Homi Bhabha
c) Vikram Sarabhai
d) A.P.J. Abdul Kalam
Answer: a

142.**What is the currency of Bangladesh?**
a) Rupee
b) Taka
c) Yuan
d) Ringgit
Answer: b

143.**Which river flows through Paris?**
a) Seine
b) Thames
c) Danube
d) Volga
Answer: a

144.**Which Indian state is known for the Hornbill Festival?**
a) Nagaland
b) Manipur
c) Mizoram
d) Assam
Answer: a

145.**Which desert in India is known as the 'Great Indian Desert'?**
a) Rann of Kutch
b) Thar Desert
c) Deccan Desert
d) Ladakh Desert
Answer: b

146.**What is the most populous city in India?**
a) New Delhi
b) Mumbai
c) Bengaluru
d) Kolkata
Answer: b

147.**What is the official language of Kerala?**
a) Tamil
b) Kannada
c) Malayalam
d) Telugu
Answer: c

148.**Which mountain range is the oldest in the world?**
a) Andes
b) Aravalli
c) Rockies
d) Himalayas
Answer: b

149.**What is the name of the first satellite launched by India?**
a) INSAT-1A
b) Bhaskara
c) Aryabhata
d) Rohini
Answer: c

150.**Which movement was launched by Mahatma Gandhi in 1930?**
a) Non-Cooperation Movement
b) Salt March
c) Quit India Movement
d) Civil Disobedience Movement
Answer: b

151.**Which state in India is famous for its toy industry in Channapatna?**
a) Karnataka
b) Tamil Nadu
c) Andhra Pradesh
d) Telangana
Answer: a

152.**Which type of farming is also called 'slash and burn' agriculture?**
a) Terrace farming
b) Shifting cultivation
c) Plantation farming
d) Subsistence farming
Answer: b

153.**Who wrote the book 'India Wins Freedom'?**
a) Jawaharlal Nehru
b) Abul Kalam Azad
c) Mahatma Gandhi
d) B.R. Ambedkar
Answer: b
154.**Which is the smallest union territory of India by area?**
a) Lakshadweep

b) Puducherry
c) Daman and Diu
d) Chandigarh
Answer: a
155.**Which state in India is known as the 'Apple State'?**
a) Uttarakhand
b) Himachal Pradesh
c) Jammu and Kashmir
d) Sikkim
Answer: b
156.**What is the term for an area drained by a river and its tributaries?**
a) Delta
b) Basin
c) Plateau
d) Estuary
Answer: b
157.**Which Article of the Indian Constitution abolishes titles?**
a) Article 17
b) Article 18
c) Article 19
d) Article 20
Answer: b
158.**Who was the last Viceroy of British India?**
a) Lord Curzon
b) Lord Wavell
c) Lord Mountbatten
d) Lord Canning
Answer: c
159.**Which port city in India is known as the 'City of Joy'?**
a) Mumbai
b) Kolkata
c) Chennai
d) Bengaluru
Answer: b
160.**Which Indian freedom fighter is associated with the slogan 'Inquilab Zindabad'?**
a) Bhagat Singh
b) Subhash Chandra Bose
c) Mahatma Gandhi
d) Bal Gangadhar Tilak
Answer: a
161.**Which battle marked the beginning of British rule in India?**
a) Battle of Plassey
b) Battle of Buxar
c) First Anglo-Mysore War
d) Battle of Panipat
Answer: a

162.**What is the largest freshwater lake in India?**
a) Chilika Lake
b) Wular Lake
c) Dal Lake
d) Sambhar Lake
Answer: b
163.**Which national park in India is famous for Bengal tigers?**
a) Kaziranga National Park
b) Jim Corbett National Park
c) Gir Forest National Park
d) Sundarbans National Park
Answer: b
164.**Which Indian scientist invented the concept of zero?**
a) Aryabhata
b) Bhaskara I
c) Varahamihira
d) Brahmagupta
Answer: d
165.**Which river forms the largest delta in the world?**
a) Ganga-Brahmaputra
b) Amazon
c) Nile
d) Mississippi
Answer: a
166.**Which dynasty built the famous Khajuraho temples?**
a) Chola dynasty
b) Chandela dynasty
c) Gupta dynasty
d) Maurya dynasty
Answer: b
167.**Who was the founder of the Mughal Empire in India?**
a) Babur
b) Akbar
c) Humayun
d) Shah Jahan
Answer: a
168.**Which movement was launched to protest against the partition of Bengal?**
a) Non-Cooperation Movement
b) Swadeshi Movement
c) Quit India Movement
d) Civil Disobedience Movement
Answer: b
169.**Which country shares the Siachen Glacier border with India?**
a) China
b) Pakistan
c) Nepal

d) Afghanistan
Answer: b
170.**Who built the Red Fort in Delhi?**
a) Akbar
b) Shah Jahan
c) Humayun
d) Jahangir
Answer: b
171.**Which metal is the best conductor of electricity?**
a) Iron
b) Copper
c) Silver
d) Aluminum
Answer: c
172.**What is the currency of Sri Lanka?**
a) Rupee
b) Taka
c) Kyat
d) Ringgit
Answer: a
173.**Which Indian state is known for the temple city of Bhubaneswar?**
a) Odisha
b) Andhra Pradesh
c) Tamil Nadu
d) Karnataka
Answer: a
174.**What is the capital of Bangladesh?**
a) Chittagong
b) Dhaka
c) Khulna
d) Sylhet
Answer: b
175.**Who was the first woman governor of an Indian state?**
a) Sarojini Naidu
b) Indira Gandhi
c) Sucheta Kripalani
d) Pratibha Patil
Answer: a
176.**Which freedom fighter founded the Indian National Army (INA)?**
a) Bhagat Singh
b) Jawaharlal Nehru
c) Subhash Chandra Bose
d) Bal Gangadhar Tilak
Answer: c
177.**Which state in India is known for its Kathakali dance?**
a) Tamil Nadu

b) Kerala
c) Karnataka
d) Andhra Pradesh
Answer: b
178.**Which river is known as the 'Lifeline of Madhya Pradesh'?**
a) Narmada
b) Godavari
c) Krishna
d) Tapi
Answer: a
179.**What is the main crop grown during the Rabi season in India?**
a) Rice
b) Wheat
c) Maize
d) Jute
Answer: b
180.**What is the national animal of India?**
a) Lion
b) Elephant
c) Bengal Tiger
d) Peacock
Answer: c
181.**Which Indian city is famous for the Golden Temple?**
a) Varanasi
b) Amritsar
c) Patna
d) Chandigarh
Answer: b
182.**Which freedom fighter is called the 'Nightingale of India'?**
a) Sarojini Naidu
b) Annie Besant
c) Indira Gandhi
d) Sucheta Kripalani
Answer: a
183.**Who wrote the national anthem of India?**
a) Rabindranath Tagore
b) Bankim Chandra Chatterjee
c) Mahatma Gandhi
d) Subhash Chandra Bose
Answer: a
184.**Which is the oldest stock exchange in India?**
a) Bombay Stock Exchange (BSE)
b) National Stock Exchange (NSE)
c) Calcutta Stock Exchange
d) Bangalore Stock Exchange
Answer: a

185.**Which Article of the Indian Constitution deals with the right to equality?**
a) Article 14
b) Article 17
c) Article 19
d) Article 21
Answer: a
186.**Which dam is built on the Mahanadi River?**
a) Hirakud Dam
b) Bhakra Dam
c) Sardar Sarovar Dam
d) Tehri Dam
Answer: a
187.**What is the full form of ISRO?**
a) Indian Scientific Research Organization
b) Indian Space Research Organization
c) International Space Research Organization
d) Indian Satellite Research Organization
Answer: b
188.**Which is the largest saltwater lake in India?**
a) Chilika Lake
b) Wular Lake
c) Dal Lake
d) Sambhar Lake
Answer: a
189.**Which festival is known as the 'Festival of Colours'?**
a) Diwali
b) Holi
c) Baisakhi
d) Dussehra
Answer: b
190.**Which type of soil is most suitable for cotton cultivation?**
a) Alluvial soil
b) Black soil
c) Red soil
d) Laterite soil
Answer: b
191.**Which river flows through the city of Kolkata?**
a) Ganga
b) Yamuna
c) Brahmaputra
d) Hooghly
Answer: d
192.**Who was the first Indian astronaut to go to space?**
a) Kalpana Chawla
b) Sunita Williams
c) Rakesh Sharma

d) Vikram Sarabhai
Answer: c
193.**Which place in India receives the highest rainfall?**
a) Mawsynram
b) Cherrapunji
c) Shillong
d) Darjeeling
Answer: a
194.**What is the largest gland in the human body?**
a) Liver
b) Pancreas
c) Kidney
d) Heart
Answer: a
195.**Which mountain pass connects India and Afghanistan?**
a) Khyber Pass
b) Rohtang Pass
c) Shipki La Pass
d) Nathu La Pass
Answer: a
196.**Which battle ended the rule of the Marathas in India?**
a) Battle of Plassey
b) Battle of Buxar
c) Third Battle of Panipat
d) First Anglo-Mysore War
Answer: c
197.**Who was the first Indian to win the Nobel Prize?**
a) Rabindranath Tagore
b) C.V. Raman
c) Amartya Sen
d) Mother Teresa
Answer: a
198.**Which crop is known as the 'Golden Fiber'?**
a) Jute
b) Cotton
c) Silk
d) Wool
Answer: a
199.**What is the southernmost point of India?**
a) Kanyakumari
b) Indira Point
c) Rameshwaram
d) Point Calimere
Answer: b

200.**Which Indian monument is known as the 'Symbol of Love'?**
a) Qutub Minar
b) Taj Mahal
c) Red Fort
d) India Gate
Answer: b

Printed at Repro India Ltd.